PIPPIN

A Musical Comedy by
ROGER O. HIRSON

Music and Lyrics by
STEPHEN SCHWARTZ

 A BARD BOOK/PUBLISHED BY AVON BOOKS

AVON BOOKS
A division of
The Hearst Corporation
959 Eighth Avenue
New York, New York 10019

First Bard Printing, April, 1977

BARD TRADEMARK REG. U.S. PAT. OFF. AND IN
OTHER COUNTRIES, MARCA REGISTRADA, HECHO EN
U.S.A.

Printed in the U.S.A.

44,633

ROGER O. HIRSON writes for the theatre, television, and motion pictures. He is the author of the plays JOURNEY TO THE DAY and WORLD WAR 2½, both of which have been produced in New York. He wrote the book for the musical WALKING HAPPY. A graduate of Yale, he worked as a newspaper reporter before becoming one of the most prolific contributors to television's major dramatic shows. He describes his collaboration with Stephen Schwartz as "both an education and a constant source of pleasure."

STEPHEN SCHWARTZ became the first composer in Broadway history to have three hits running in New York at the same time when THE MAGIC SHOW opened in the summer of 1974, joining the long-running GODSPELL and PIPPIN. His other credits include the title song for BUTTERFLIES ARE FREE and, in collaboration with Leonard Bernstein, the English texts for MASS.

A hardcover edition of PIPPIN is available in a $5.95 edition published by Drama Book Specialists (Publishers), New York.

PIPPIN was first presented on October 23, 1972 by
Stuart Ostrow at the Imperial Theatre in New York
City with the following cast:

LEADING PLAYER	Ben Vereen
PIPPIN	John Rubenstein
CHARLES	Eric Berry
LEWIS	Christopher Chadman
FASTRADA	Leland Palmer
MUSICIAN	John Mineo
THE HEAD	Roger Hamilton
BERTHE	Irene Ryan
BEGGAR	Richard Korthaze
PEASANT	Paul Solen
NOBLE	Gene Foote
FIELD MARSHALL	Roger Hamilton
CATHERINE	Jill Clayburgh
THEO	Shane Nickerson
PLAYERS	Candy Brown
	Ann Reinking, Jennifer Nairn-Smith
	Kathryn Doby, Pamela Sousa

Book by Roger O. Hirson
Music and lyrics by Stephen Schwartz
Directed and choreographed by Bob Fosse
Scenery designed by Tony Walton
Costumes by Patricia Zipprodt
Lighting by Jules Fisher
Musical direction by Stanley Lebowsky
Orchestrations by Ralph Burns
Dance arrangements by John Berkman
Sound design by Abe Jacob

MUSICAL NUMBERS

Scene 1: THE OPENING
"Magic to Do"   THE PLAYERS
"Corner of the Sky"   PIPPIN

Scene 2: HOME
"Welcome Home"   CHARLES AND PIPPIN

Scene 3: WAR
"War is a Science"   CHARLES, PIPPIN,
                                AND SOLDIERS
"Glory"   LEADING PLAYER AND SOLDIERS

Scene 4: THE FLESH
"Simple Joys"   LEADING PLAYER
"No Time at All"   BERTHE AND THE BOYS
"With You"   PIPPIN AND THE GIRLS

Scene 5: REVOLUTION
"Spread a Little Sunshine"   FASTRADA
"Morning Glow"   PIPPIN AND SOLDIERS

Scene 6: ENCOURAGEMENT
"On the Right Track"   LEADING PLAYER
                               AND PIPPIN

Scene 7: THE HEARTH
"Kind of Woman"   CATHERINE
"Extraordinary"   PIPPIN
"Love Song"   PIPPIN AND CATHERINE
"I Guess I'll Miss the Man"   CATHERINE

Scene 8: THE FINALE
"Finale"   THE PLAYERS, PIPPIN

PIPPIN

Scene 1:

THE OPENING

At the rise, the stage is filled with smoke and in total darkness except for moving hands. The hands are illuminated by a light curtain which keeps the stage in virtual darkness, so that the writhing hands exist in a strange, macabre limbo.

An orchestral vamp is accompanied by a low, crooning vocal wail.

Then, from the center of the rotating hands, the face of the LEADING PLAYER appears and is hit by a spot light. He crosses the light curtain and moves downstage to the audience and sings.

As the song progresses, we can see a bare stage populated by a group of actors. Their costumes are of an undetermined period. But they are definitely PLAYERS ... a troupe ... a theatrical caravan of some kind.

One by one, they come through the light curtain, and are hit by spot lights; until finally, they all come forward and join the song.

LEADING PLAYER   (Sings)
Join us—leave your field to flower
Join us—leave your cheese to sour
Join us—come and waste an hour or two
Doo-dle-ee-do

Journey—journey to a spot ex-
    citing, mystic and exotic
Journey—through our anecdotic revue

We've got magic to do—just for you
We've got miracle plays to play
We've got parts to perform—hearts to warm
Kings and things to take by storm
As we go along our way

FASTRADA   *(Sings)*
Intrigue—plots to bring disaster

BERTHE   *(Sings)*
Humor—handled by a master

TWO GIRLS   *(Sing)*
Romance—sex presented pastorally

LEADING PLAYER   *(Sings)*
Dee-dle-ee-dee

LEWIS   *(Sings)*
Illusion—fantasy to study

CHARLES   *(Sings)*
Battles—barbarous and bloody

LEADING PLAYER   *(Sings)*
So join us—sit where everybody can see

(The remaining PLAYERS *step through the light curtain and they all sing)*

ALL *(Sing)*
　　We've got magic to do—just for you
　　We've got miracle plays to play
　　We've got parts to perform—hearts to warm
　　Kings and things to take by storm
　　As we go along our way

(The song develops into a dance of sorts. It involves all kinds of magic tricks, etc., all the things that PLAYERS *have ever done to attract and hold an audience)*

　　We've got magic to do—just for you
　　We've got miracle plays to play
　　We've got parts to perform—hearts to warm
　　Kings and things to take by storm
　　As we go along

We got
　Magic to do
just for you
　We got magic
To do
　just for you
We got magic
　To do
just for you
　As we go
along
Our way

Our way . . .
Magic to do

Magic to play
We got
Foibles and
Fables to
Portray
As we go
Along

Our way

(After the song, the music continues under)

LEADING PLAYER This evening for your entertainment
and pleasure, we present our most mysterious and mi-
raculous tale. A stunning example of . . .

A PLAYER   Magic!

A PLAYER   And merriment!

LEADING PLAYER You will witness acts of . . .

A PLAYER   Lust!

A PLAYER   Murder!

A PLAYER   Holy war!

LEADING PLAYER And a climax, ladies and gentlemen, a climax never before seen on a public stage . . .
(A PLAYER *jumps onstage from a hidden platform on
the side of the stage. He has a lighted torch in his
hand.*) Not now . . . later . . . (*The* PLAYER *with the
torch goes. The* LEADING PLAYER *continues*) Our tale
today concerns the first-born son of Charlemagne . . .
and is entitled . . . (*The* PLAYERS *pull out a large cloth
which has been concealed in one of their costumes. It
reads:* PIPPIN: HIS LIFE AND TIMES) But, before we
begin, let me assure you that what you are about to see
is the *true* life story of Pippin. You see, there have been
many misconceptions about Pippin . . . one that he
was . . .

(*During the following a few of the* PLAYERS, *all of
whom are now hidden behind the cloth sign, come
around or from under it to deliver their lines*)

A PLAYER   A hunchback.

LEADING PLAYER   Or that he was ...

A PLAYER   Enormously tall.

LEADING PLAYER   Or that he was ...

A PLAYER   Completely bald at the age of fourteen.

(They all go back behind the sign)

LEADING PLAYER   But I beg you, cast all previous misconceptions aside. And accept what we enact for you today. *(Pause)* The life of Pippin begins ... *(There is a cry and one of the* PLAYERS *is raised above the sign with a bundle in her arms)* Pippin, as a child, showed tremendous thirst for knowledge ... *(The* WOMAN PLAYER *is lowered, and a* BOY *is held up reading a small book)* Immersed in these pursuits, the years went by quickly. *(The Boy is lowered, and* PIPPIN *is raised above the sign. He is reading a large book. He looks out at the audience and smiles as he is lowered behind the sign)* Charlemagne sent Pippin to the University of Padua ...

CHARLEMAGNE   *(Stepping to the side of the cloth)* ... and the faculty of the university granted him the special title of scholar of the house.

LEADING PLAYER   Pippin replied to this offer in his own deeply moving words ...

(The LEADING PLAYER *pulls the cloth away.* PIPPIN *is revealed. The troupe applauds, but it is a*

silent applause, and only one of the PLAYERS *actually claps.* PIPPIN *looks around, looks up, frowns slightly, then addresses the* LEADING PLAYER)

PIPPIN   Could I have some more lights, please?

(LEADING PLAYER *claps his hands and a spot light hits* PIPPIN)

PIPPIN   Thank you. Gentle tutors ... respected members of the faculty ... I'm very grateful for the knowledge that you have given me. But I'm afraid what I'm looking for can't be found in books ...

LEADING PLAYER   And Pippin made a promise ...

PIPPIN   I promise not to waste my life in commonplace, ordinary pursuits.

A PLAYER   *(Sarcastically)*   Terrific.

(The other PLAYERS *mumble praise)*

PIPPIN   You see I know there is something ...

LEADING PLAYER   Something fulfilling? Completely fulfilling ...

PIPPIN   Yes. That's it. Something completely fulfilling.

A PLAYER   Oh, fantastic.

PIPPIN   And I'm going to find it ...

(Underscoring begins)

PIPPIN   I'm not exactly sure what I want to do . . . or where I want to go . . .

(Sings)

Everything has its season
Everything has its time
Show me a reason and I'll soon show you a rhyme
Cats fit on the window sill
Children fit in the snow
Why do I feel I don't fit in anywhere I go?

Rivers belong where they can ramble
Eagles belong where they can fly
I've got to be where my spirit can run free
Got to find my corner of the sky

Every man has his daydreams
Every man has his goal
People like the way dreams have of sticking to the
    soul
Thunderclouds have their lightning
Nightingales have their song
And don't you see I want my life to be something
    more than long . . .

Rivers belong where they can ramble
Eagles belong where they can fly
I've got to be where my spirit can run free
Got to find my corner of the sky

So many men seem destined
To settle for something small
But I won't rest until I know I'll have it all
So don't ask where I'm going

Just listen when I'm gone
And far away you'll hear me singing softly to the
    dawn:

Rivers belong where they can ramble
Eagles belong where they can fly
I've got to be where my spirit can run free
Got to find my corner
Of the sky . . .

(After the song, everyone applauds in eerie slow-motion. When the music begins again, they bow and begin to move off, taking PIPPIN *with them)*

LEADING PLAYER   *(Sings)*
Journey—journey to a spot ex-
   citing, mystic, and exotic
Journey—through our anecdotic revue

(The music continues. As it does, the LEADING PLAYER *performs a trick in which he makes a red scarf disappear in his hand. He then points down to the center of the stage. As he does, a spot light hits the center of the stage, and the* LEADING PLAYER *crosses to the light and begins to pull what seems to be the same red scarf out of the floor. As it gets larger and larger one sees it is attached to the palace portal which now rises entirely out of the floor, magically and majestically. It is the full length of the stage. The* PLAYERS *enter with step units completing the magic change. When they are finished, they bow to the audience and go. The* LEADING PLAYER *indicates the new set to the audience and to* PIPPIN *who has entered and is excitedly watching the transformation)*

LEADING PLAYER The royal court of Charles the
Great . . .

*(He bows to the audience and squeezes out his
own arc.* PIPPIN *addresses the audience)*

Scene 2:

HOME

PIPPIN   The first day I was home from Padua my father sent me a horse. The second day he sent me a falcon. The third day I went hunting. And on the fourth day, my father finally came himself.

   (There is a flash of fire, and CHARLEMAGNE *appears)*

LEADING PLAYER   Enter ... Charlemagne.

CHARLES   This part is to be portrayed by an actor of enormous power.

LEADING PLAYER   A giant on the battlefield and in the bedroom.

CHARLES   Oh, thank you so much.

LEADING PLAYER   You're welcome.

   (He goes)

CHARLES   *(Moving to* PIPPIN*)* Good morning.

PIPPIN   *(Kneeling)* Good morning, sir.

(CHARLES *opens his arms to* PIPPIN *and they embrace*)

CHARLES   Well, welcome home, son ... well ...

(*Father and son look at each other in embarrassment*)

CHARLES   (*Sings*)
Hello, son.

PIPPIN   (*Sings*)
Hello.

CHARLES   (*Sings*)
You look thinner.

PIPPIN   (*Sings*)
I know.

CHARLES   (*Sings*)
So, son

PIPPIN   (*Sings*)
So ...

CHARLES   (*Sings*)
Last night didn't you miss dinner?

PIPPIN   No.

CHARLES   Oh. Well, how did things go in Padua?

PIPPIN   Very well, sir, some of my tutors ...

CHARLES *(Interrupting* PIPPIN*)* Good ... good. I'm a great believer in education.

PIPPIN   And yet you have become the most powerful man in the world without it.

CHARLES   The most powerful man in the world? Oh, Pippin, don't exaggerate. What about the Pope?

PIPPIN   I rank you ahead of the Pope, sir.

CHARLES   I happen to agree with you. But the world I grew up in was simpler. The sword solved every problem. Tomorrow is for you.

PIPPIN   But it's still today.

CHARLES   But for how long? Pippin, sunrise and sunset are similar, but not identical.

(Action freezes on CHARLES *and* PIPPIN. *The* LEADING PLAYER *appears)*

LEADING PLAYER   Enter Lewis ... (LEWIS *jumps up from the side. As the* LEADING PLAYER *introduces him, he strikes a series of characteristically masculine poses to show off his muscles)* Pippin's half-brother ... and after Pippin, heir to the throne. Addicted to the physical, Lewis loves weight lifting ... Lewis loves wrestling ... but most of all ... Lewis loves Lewis.

*(*LEWIS *winks at the audience and then crosses the stage swinging his sword, as if he were attacking something.* CHARLES *and* PIPPIN *are again in the scene)*

LEWIS   Hah! Hah! Hah! Hah!

PIPPIN   Well done, brother.

LEWIS   Well done? Ha! That was magnificent! Did you know this arm slew twenty Frisians last year? And it's going to slay even more Visigoths.

PIPPIN   You mean you're going to war against the Visigoths?

LEWIS   Uh huh. That's the next one. It's going to be a glorious campaign. And oh—those Visigoth women. I don't mean to shock your bookish sensibilities.

PIPPIN   I'm only shocked that you're interested in women now.

(The action freezes and once more the LEADING PLAYER *appears, high up on the portal)*

LEADING PLAYER   Enter ... Fastrada.

(As he speaks, a black tab is taken up and FASTRADA *is revealed standing in the light)*

LEADING PLAYER   Pippin's step-mother. Devious ... crafty, cunning, untrustworthy ... but a warm and wonderful mother. Dedicated to gaining the throne for her darling son, Lewis.

(Action begins, FASTRADA *comes downstage to* LEWIS)

FASTRADA   Lewis! Lewis! Guess what Mommy has for you ... Surprise!

(She gives LEWIS *a breastplate)*

LEWIS Oh, thank you, Mother. Look at this! Isn't it a beauty?

PIPPIN It really *is* beautiful.

FASTRADA Welcome home, Pippin. *(Blowing a kiss to* CHARLES) My darling.

LEWIS Can you imagine how I'll shine in the sun?

  (FASTRADA *lovingly helps* LEWIS *put on the breast-plate)*

FASTRADA Darling, you look beautiful. Doesn't he, Charles? (LEWIS *begins to strut around, showing off his new armor)* Oh Pippin, stand up straight. Didn't they teach you posture at Padua?

PIPPIN I failed posture.

  (He slumps deliberately)

FASTRADA Notice how straight Lewis stands ...

PIPPIN Oh, yes, he's a real straightstander ... no question about that.

LEWIS Look how I shine. *(Crosses with swordplay)* Hah, Visigoths!

  (Exits)

FASTRADA We're so proud of Lewis, aren't we, dear?
Oh, my darling, before I forget, the royal treasurer in-
forms me I've overdrawn my allowance account.

CHARLES You're overdrawn again . . .?

FASTRADA Now, now, my lord, don't be angry with
me. You know how confused I get about money. After
all, I am just an ordinary housewife and mother . . .
(To audience) . . . just like all you housewives and
mothers out there.

  (She goes)

CHARLES You know, sometimes I wonder if the fornicating I'm getting is worth the fornicating I'm getting.
(Turns to PIPPIN*)* Well, son, now we can have our
talk. How've things been going with you?

PIPPIN Well, not very well. Father, there were a lot
of . . .

CHARLES *(Interrupting him, sings)*
  Welcome home, son, welcome home
  I'm so glad to hear there's nothing wrong
  Welcome home son, glad you're home
  Will you be staying long?

PIPPIN Well. That's what I wanted to talk to you
about, Father. I wanted to ask you . . .

CHARLES *(Going on, sings)*
  Welcome home, son, welcome home
  Well, I've got to go, it's almost noon

PIPPIN   *(Trying to break through)* But Father . . .

CHARLES   *(Sings)*
  Welcome home, son, glad you're home
  We'll talk again soon . . .
  (Speaks) Keep busy while you're here. Why don't you take that falcon and horse I gave you and go hunting?

PIPPIN   Good idea. Thank you, Sir.

CHARLES   *(Starts off, then turns)* Oh, Pippin . . .

PIPPIN   Yes, Sir?

CHARLES   *(Sings)*
  One more thought I would impart is . . .
  I may blush, but I'll be frank . . .

PIPPIN   *(Sings)*
  Do, Sir . . .

CHARLES   *(A pause, then nothing but a cliché, sings)*
Home is where the heart is. *(To himself)* Why did I say that?

PIPPIN   *(Sings)*
Thank you, sir. *(To himself)* Why did he say that? (CHARLES *goes. Music begins)* The preparations for the Visigoth campaign were reaching a peak. Marksmen tested themselves against the butts. *(Arrows fly across the stage)* Swordsmen tested themselves against each other. *(Upstage, swordsmen duel)* The panoply of war was being assembled. The sights and sounds of glory were in the air.

SOLDIERS *(Scream)* Glory!

  (Exit)

PIPPIN Glory's in the air! And what am I doing?
Nothing.

  (LEADING PLAYER *enters, wearing a helmet and
carrying weapons*)

LEADING PLAYER *(Handing* PIPPIN *a sword)* Your
sword, sir. *(Looks more closely)* Oh, excuse me. I
thought you were a warrior.

PIPPIN No, no, no, wait. I'll keep it.

LEADING PLAYER But you're not one of us ...

PIPPIN I'm Prince Pippin.

LEADING PLAYER Who?

PIPPIN Prince Pippin. One day I will be king.
(Rises on tiptoes)

LEADING PLAYER Oh.

  (LEADING PLAYER *goes.*)
  (PIPPIN *looks at the sword and lunges with it*)

PIPPIN Hah, Visigoths! *(To audience)* I think I'm
going to talk to my father.

  (The set changes to CHARLES' *court. Lights up on*
CHARLES *as he enters)*

FEMALE COURTIER The royal court of Charles the Great, emperor of the Holy Roman empire . . .

CHARLES And a giant in the bedroom . . .

COURTIER And a giant in the bedroom . . . *(Indicating with a "so so" gesture of her hand that* CHARLES *isn't much of a giant)* . . . is prepared to hear petitions.

   (Lights up on a BARON*)*

BARON Oh, great leader, blessed by God, sent to us from Heaven to protect us from the Infidel . . .

CHARLES *(Impatient)* Oh, what is it?

BARON I beseech you to reduce my levy of footsoldiers, cattle and wheat. Due to a famine . . .

CHARLES *(Interrupting)* Denied. Next.

BARON But, sire, my cattle are dying and my fields are barren . . .

CHARLES Denied. Next.

BARON But, sire, that is unjust and tyrannical. I object.

CHARLES Take that man away and hang him! *(The* LEADING PLAYER *steps from behind the staircase and places the noose around the* BARON'S *neck)* Next!

PETITIONER *(Stepping forward)* Oh, great leader, blessed by God, sent to us from Heaven . . .

CHARLES Oh, no. Not all that bullshit again. Out!
Out! Everybody out! Council is dismissed.

PIPPIN Wait! Father . . .

CHARLES Denied. Next.

PIPPIN Father, it's me.

CHARLES Oh, Pippin . . . What is it?

PIPPIN I know what I want to do now.

CHARLES Good. Good.

PIPPIN I want to be a soldier.

CHARLES What!

PIPPIN Yes, I want to join you in your campaign
against the Visigoths.

CHARLES Denied.

PIPPIN But that's not fair.

CHARLES To an emperor fairness is irrelevant.

PIPPIN You're taking Lewis.

CHARLES *(Coming down from his throne)* Yes, well,
your brother Lewis is an ideal soldier. He is strong and
stupid. You, on the other hand, are educated.

PIPPIN   But, I'm your oldest son. That means I might be king one day. Fighting wars is an important part of being king, isn't it?

CHARLES   Fighting wars is the *most* important part of being king. I mean after all, the Pope and I have dedicated ourselves to bringing Christianity to the entire world . . .

PIPPIN   Well, that's what I'm talking about. You're dedicated to something, and I just want to be dedicated to something, too . . . with all my heart and soul . . . and whatever it is, I want to do it as well as I possibly can. Otherwise, my life won't have any meaning at all.

CHARLES   Oh, you want your life to have meaning, do you?

PIPPIN   Yes, I do.

CHARLES   Well, that's very ambitious of you, Pippin.

PIPPIN   Father, stop all this . . . bullshit . . . and take me with you.

CHARLES   (*Surprised at* PIPPIN'S *language*) Oh, ho, ho. (*A moment*) Very well, then. Get yourself a decent helmet and come along. (CHARLES *goes. The* LEADING PLAYER *enters from the wings and puts a helmet on* PIPPIN'S *head.* PIPPIN *looks at the* LEADING PLAYER)

PIPPIN   I'm a soldier.

LEADING PLAYER   Right.

PIPPIN Me, a warrior. Finally, a chance to be part of something important. A chance to use my sword ... my arm ... and maybe, even my blood ...

(The drum roll which has been under all this becomes intense)

A SOLDIER Glory!

A SOLDIER Glory!

(The stage begins to fill with MEN *in full battle regalia. There is a short dance as the set changes from court to the tent of* CHARLEMAGNE*)*

Scene 3:

WAR

CHARLES Gentlemen, be seated. Map! *(A map is lowered from the flies)* Well, gentlemen, it's been a long, hard march. This is where we are . . . *(Indicating on the map)* Here. Tomorrow morning at sunrise we go against the Visigoths.

PIPPIN *(Jumping to his feet)* Hah, Visigoths!

CHARLES Pippin, sit down. (PIPPIN *sits*) Now the main factor in tomorrow's battle is the terrain. So look at this map. Study it. Remember it.

PIPPIN Father, why can't we just go out there and slaughter them?

CHARLES You spoke, Pippin?

PIPPIN Since we're braver and stronger and have God on our side, can't we just go out there and kill at will?

CHARLES War is a science, Pippin.

PIPPIN That takes half the fun out of it right there.

CHARLES   There's plenty of fun when you win.

   (Sings)

War is a science
With rules to be applied
Which good soldiers appreciate
Recall and recapitulate
Before they go to decimate
The other side
   (Speaks) Now, gentlemen, this is the plan for to-
morrow's skirmish.

   (Sings)

The army of the enemy is stationed on the hill
So we've got to get them down here, and this is
   how we will
Our men in the ravine (that's this area in green)
Will move across the valley where they plainly
   can be seen
And the enemy (in blue) will undoubtedly pursue
For that's what you depend upon an enemy to do.

Then to guarantee their folly
We'll bring bowmen into play
Who will fire just one volley
And retire to point "A".

And then, and then,
And gentlemen, and then ...

PIPPIN   *(Sings)*
And then the men go marching out into the fray
Conquering the enemy and carrying the day
Hark! The blood is pounding in our ears
Jubilations! We can hear a grateful nation's cheers!

CHARLES   Pippin, sit down immediately.

PIPPIN   I'm sorry, Father. I just got carried away.

  (PIPPIN *sits*)

CHARLES   *(Long, disapproving look at* PIPPIN*)* Now
where was I? Ah, yes ...

  (Sings)

  War is a science
  A breeding ground for brains
  For though I cannot write my name
  The men whose pens have brought them fame
  Write endless paragraphs explaining
  My campaigns

  Now when the foe see our soldiers marching
      through the lea
  They will mount a charge and meet us at the point
      I've labelled "B"
  And their bowmen on the hill (in yellow on the map)
  Will leave their posts to join the rest and fall
      into our trap
  Then we'll cut off reinforcements and retreat of any
      kind
  Bearing principles of enfilade and defilade in mind.

  And if all the ploys we pick to rea-
      lly work to bring to pass occur
  We won't have just a victory
  We'll have ourselves a massacre

  And then, and then
  And gentlemen, and then ...

PIPPIN   *(Sings)*
   And then the men go marching out into the fray
   Conquering the enemy and carrying the day
   Hark! The blood is pounding in our ears
   Jubilations! We can hear a grateful nation's . . .

CHARLES   Pippin . . . !

PIPPIN   I'm sorry, Father. It won't happen again.

CHARLES   *(Looks at* PIPPIN *and shakes his head)* In conclusion, gentlemen . . .

   (Sings)

   Now listen to me closely, I'll endeavor to explain
   What separates a Charlatan from a Charlemagne
   A rule confessed by generals illustrious and various
   Though pompous as a Pompey or daring as a Darius
   A simple rule that every great man learns by heart
   It's smarter to be lucky than it's lucky to be smart.

   But if the fates feel frivolous
   And all our plans they smother
   Well, suppose this war does shrivel us
   They'll always be another!

   And then . . .

ALL   *(Sing)*
   And then . . .

CHARLES   *(Sings)*
   And gentlemen, and then . . .
     (Speaks) Now . . . gentlemen . . . now!

(The SOLDIERS *rise from the benches with swords in hand, and the music changes to a softshoe which the* SOLDIERS *proceed to do as they sing)*

SOLDIERS   *(Sing)*
And then the men go marching out into the fray
Conquering the enemy and carrying the day
Hark! The blood is pounding in our ears!
Jubilations!
We can hear a grateful nation's cheers!

(They exit. CHARLES, PIPPIN, *and* LEWIS *are alone on stage. During the first part of the following scene, the* SOLDIERS *come back onstage and take out the benches)*

CHARLES   *(Confronting* PIPPIN*)* Pippin, I find your attitude very disturbing.

PIPPIN   Oh, Father, I'm sorry. It was just all that talk about enfilade and defilade . . .

CHARLES   Now remember this, Pippin . . . the Visigoth king across the valley is talking about enfilade and defilade, too. That's the way it's done.

PIPPIN   I'll know better next time.

CHARLES   I certainly hope so. Well, there's just one other thing. I always like to spend the night before battle praying. I would like my two sons to join me. *(*CHARLES *kneels.* LEWIS *and* PIPPIN *kneel on either side of him)* Oh God, we who fight in your name and in the name of your Son, ask for victory in combat tomorrow . . .

PIPPIN Father, is the Visigoth king praying for victory, too?

CHARLES Oh yes. Old King Aleric is one of the best prayers in the business.

(LEADING PLAYER *enters as a drum roll is heard*)

CHARLES *(Continues)* Lewis ... Pippin ... It's time.

LEWIS You're going to be very proud of me, Father.

(CHARLES *looks at* PIPPIN)

PIPPIN I will try not to disgrace you, sir.

CHARLES Very well, follow me.

(CHARLES, LEWIS, *and* PIPPIN *march off. The* LEADING PLAYER *is alone on stage. The music begins and he sings*)

LEADING PLAYER *(Sings)*
Battles, barbarous and bloody

(*He's thrown a hat and a cane from offstage which he puts on*)

Glory! Glory!
Glory! Glory!
Praise be to Charles our lord
Triumphant is his sword.
Allegiance is his word.
Glory! Glory!
Glory! Glory!

Blood!

Blood is red as sunset.
Blood is warmer than wine
Warmer than wine.
The taste of salty summer brine.

(*The* SOLDIERS *enter in a battle formation behind the* LEADING PLAYER)

Steel!

ALL   (*Sing*)
Steel is cold as moonlight
Steel is sharper than sight
Sharper than sight
The touch of bitter winter white

SOLDIERS   (*Sing*)
Shout it out from the highest tower
Shout it out in the darkest hour
Charlemagne, you lead us on to

ALL   (*Sing*)
Power!

LEADING PLAYER   (*Sings*)
War!

LEADING PLAYER   (*Sings*)   SOLDIERS   (*Sing*)
War is strict as Jesus   War
War is finer than spring   War

LEADING PLAYER and 2 SOLDIERS   (*Sing*)
Service to Christ and to our

ALL *(Sing)*
    King.
    Shout it out from the highest tower
    Shout it out in the darkest hour
    Charlemagne, you lead us on to power . . .

(The LEADING PLAYER *and* TWO SOLDIERS *do a dance behind which killings are taking place in limbo. At one point,* PIPPIN *crosses the stage with blood on his hand, and a* SOLDIER *crosses with a head on a pike-staff)*

LEADING PLAYER *(When the dance is at an end)* Ta dum.

(The LEADING PLAYER *is alone on stage. He comes down and sits on the platform, legs crossed, sings)*

War is strict as Jesus

(The stage is littered with limbs and bodies and heads, etc.)

War is finer than spring

(More limbs are thrown on stage. The SOLDIERS *enter and begin to go through the bodies looking for valuables. The* LEADING PLAYER *rises and moves toward them)*

ALL *(Sing)*
    The gates of heaven await
    Thrown wide by Charles the great
    We follow him through by serving his state

(The shadow of CHARLES *is projected on a drop behind them, larger than life)*

ALL   *(Sing)*
   Glory! Glory!
   Glory! Glory!
   Glory!
   Yeah!

CHARLES   We've won.

SOLDIERS   We've won.

(The SOLDIERS *begin to walk among the bodies)*

LEWIS   I killed at least twenty-five of them myself, Father.

CHARLES   Yes, you and Pippin both did very well. Well, now we rape and sack. (PIPPIN *who has entered looks dubious at the prospect)* Oh yes, it's required. We also have to sing. That's absolutely essential to victory . . .

(Music starts and the SOLDIERS *dance into formation and dance off during the following)*

CHARLES	SOLDIERS *(Sing)*
Fall to, men	And then the men go
Eat. Drink. Rape.	marching out into the fray
Give thanks to God	Conquering the enemy and
who granted us	carrying the day
this . . . victory	Hark! The blood is pound-
	ing in our ears
	Jubilation! We can hear a
	grateful nation cheer!

(PIPPIN *is alone on stage. He moves among the dismembered pieces*)

PIPPIN *(Seeing a head)* I suppose it's a little late to wonder who this man was.

HEAD It is a little late. But as long as you're interested, I'm just a common man, a Visigoth, but a good man ... a very good man.

PIPPIN You're also a very lucky man. You've had the privilege of dying for your king.

HEAD Words fail me.

CHARLES *(Entering and going upstage)* Pippin, you aren't celebrating. And you there, get all this litter cleared away.

(THREE STREETCLEANERS *come on with a round cart. They begin to pick up and sweep away the limbs, bodies, etc.*)

PIPPIN *(To the* HEAD*)* You know of course, dying in battle like this, you'll be going straight to Valhalla ... or wherever you Infidels go, won't you?

HEAD Absolutely. The King has assured us personally. But this waiting around's got me edgy.

PIPPIN This wasn't your first battle, was it?

HEAD No. My third.

PIPPIN Well, then maybe you could tell me, how did this battle compare with your other two?

HEAD Well, unless you get killed, one battle's pretty much like another.

PIPPIN I was afraid you'd say that.

CHARLES Pippin! What's the matter? What are you doing?

(A STREETCLEANER *comes downstage to the* HEAD *and picks it up and carries it back to his cart)*

PIPPIN *(To the* HEAD*)* I hope you get to Valhalla soon . . .

HEAD Hope you get to Heaven . . .

*(*STREETCLEANER *drops the* HEAD *into his cart and goes)*

PIPPIN Oh, I will.

CHARLES *(Upstage)* Pippin, this is embarrassing. A victory celebration and my own son not joining in.

PIPPIN *(Softly)* Sorry, Father. You'll have to get used to victory celebrations without me. *(After a moment, to the audience)* I thought there'd be more plumes . . .

(Then softly, sings)

Rivers belong where they can ramble
Eagles belong where they can fly
I've got to be where my spirit can run free
Got to find my corner of the sky . . .

(The LEADING PLAYER *and* A PLAYER *with a guitar enter from upstage)*

Scene 4:

THE FLESH

LEADING PLAYER   *(Sings)*
Well, I'll sing you the story of a sorrowful lad
Had everything he wanted, didn't want what he had
He had wealth and pelf and fame and name and all
of that noise
But he didn't have none of those simple joys
His life seemed purposeless and flat
Aren't you glad you don't feel like that?

(PIPPIN *runs offstage*)

So he ran from all the deeds he'd done, he ran from
things he'd just begun
He ran from himself, now that's mighty far to run
Out into the country where he played as a boy
'Cause he knew he had to find him some simple joy
He wanted some place warm and green
We all could use a change of scene

(The set changes into a country setting, grass, trees, and sun)

Sweet summer evenings, hot wine and bread
Sharing your supper, sharing your bed
Simple joys have a simple voice:

It says why not go ahead?
Wouldn't you rather be a left-handed flea
Or a crab on a slab at the bottom of the sea
Than a man who never learns how to be free
Not till he's cold and dead.

Sweet summer evenings so full of sound
Gaining a lover, gaining a pound
Simple joys have a simple voice
It says: take a look around
And wouldn't you rather be a left-handed flea
A crab on a slab at the bottom of the sea
Or a newt on the root of a banyan tree
Than a man who never learns how to be free
Not till he's underground
   (Speaks) Enter . . . Berthe *(A chair turns around and reveals* BERTHE*)* Pippin's grandmother; warm, strong . . .

BERTHE   Still attractive . . .

LEADING PLAYER   Still attractive. Charlemagne's mother . . . Now living in the country where she enjoys those . . .

   (Sings)

Sweet summer evenings, sapphire skies
Feasting her belly
Feasting her eyes
Simple joys have a simple voice
It says time is living's prize
And wouldn't you
Rather be a left-handed flea
A crab on a slab at the bottom of the sea

A newt on the root of a banyan tree
Or a fig on a twig in Galilee
Then a man who never learns how to be free
Not till the day
Not till the day
Not till the day
Not till the day he dies!
Na na na na na na na na na na na na na na na

(He exits, and as he does PIPPIN *enters)*

PIPPIN   Berthe . . .

BERTHE   *(Having trouble with her needlework)*
Damn! I hate needlepoint!

PIPPIN   Berthe . . .

BERTHE   Yes . . .? What is it . . .?

PIPPIN   It's me. Pippin.

BERTHE   Pippin . . . Pippin . . .? Oh, Pippin, I can't
believe it. *(She holds out her arms.* PIPPIN *embraces
her)* Oh, how good it is to hold you . . . to hold you
like I used to when you were a little boy. Remember,
Pippin?

PIPPIN   Well of course I remember. That's why I came
here.

BERTHE   Oh Pippin, you look terrible. You need
some fresh air . . . some sun . . . and good food . . .
(Then with a twinkle) . . . some frolicking . . .

PIPPIN   Grandma, you haven't changed a bit.

BERTHE   But you have, Pippin. Now something is the matter . . . what have you been doing with yourself?

PIPPIN   I went to war, Grandma.

BERTHE   No wonder you look so terrible. Men and their wars. Sometimes I think men raise flags when they can't get anything else up.

PIPPIN   Grandma, sometimes you really say shocking things.

BERTHE   I try my best. But Pippin, what's wrong?

PIPPIN   I don't know, Grandma. I feel empty and vacant . . .

BERTHE   Empty and vacant? Now Pippin. You listen to me . . . you're going to hear something very . . . *(Indicating quotes)* . . . "wise". Now don't take life so seriously. Just take things as they come along. Don't do too much planning, and don't do too much thinking. How's that for wisdom so far?

PIPPIN   *(Tentative)* Well, frankly, Grandma, it sounds pretty dull . . .

BERTHE   It'll sound better with music . . . maestro . . .

  (Sings)

  When you are as old as I, my dear
  And I hope that you never are

You will woefully wonder why, my dear
Through your cataracts and catarrh
You could squander away or sequester
A drop of a precious year
For when your best days are yester
The rest 're twice as dear . . .

What good is a field on a fine summer night
If you sit all alone with the weeds?
Or a succulent pear if with each juicy bite
You spit out your teeth with the seeds?
Before it's too late stop trying to wait
For fortune and fate you're secure of
For there's one thing to be sure of, mate:
There's nothing to be sure of.

Oh, it's time to start livin'
Time to take a little from this world we're given
Time to take time, cause Spring will turn to Fall
In just no time at all . . .

(PIPPIN *jumps to his feet*)

PIPPIN But Grandma, it's *time* that I'm worried about.

BERTHE Now you sit down. And don't say anything until I'm finished. I've got three more choruses to do. But you all can join in with me if you wish . . . *(To audience)* And that goes for all of you out there, too. But just the choruses, the verses are all mine.

(Sings)

I've never wondered if I was afraid
When there was a challenge to take

I never thought about how much I weighed
When there was still one piece of cake
Maybe it's meant the hours I've spent
Feeling broken and bent and unwell
But there's still no cure so Heaven-sent
As the chance to raise some hell.

(The BOYS join her. A song sheet is lowered behind her, and the words of the song are delineated by a bouncing ball of light)

Everybody . . .

ALL! *(Sing)*
Oh, it's time to start livin'
Time to take a little from the world we're given
Time to take time, for Spring will turn to Fall
In just no time at all

BERTHE   Verse! *(Sings)*
Now when the drearies do attack
And a siege of the sads begins
I throw these regal shoulders back
And lift these noble chins

Give me a man who is handsome and strong
Someone who's stalwart and steady
Give me a night that's romantic and long
Then give me a month to get ready
Now I could waylay some aging roue
And persuade him to play in some cranny
But it's hard to believe you're being led astray
By a man who calls you Granny

(Speaks)

One more time! Come on boys! And this time let's
hear it from everybody! One! Two! Three! Four!

ALL   *(Sing)*
    Oh, it's time to start livin'

    (BERTHE *encourages the audience to sing along.*
    She shouts "Everybody")

    Time to take a little from the world we've given
    Time to take time, for Spring will turn to Fall
    In just no time at all

BERTHE   Come on! You ought to know it by now!

ALL   *(Sing)*
    Oh, it's time to start livin'
    Time to take a little from the world we're given
    Time to take time, for Spring will turn to Fall
    In just no time at all

BERTHE   Out! Out!

    (Sings)

    Sages tweet that age is sweet
    Good deeds and good work earn you laurels
    But what could make you feel more obsolete
    Than being noted for your morals?

    Here is a secret I never have told
    Maybe you'll understand why
    I believe if I refuse to grow old
    I can stay young till I die
    Now, I've known the fears of sixty-six years

I've had troubles and tears by the score
But the only thing I'd trade them for
Is sixty-seven more . . .

ALL   *(Sing)*
Oh, it's time to start . . .

BERTHE   *(Stopping the* BOYS *and audience from singing)* Aaah! *(To the man in the light booth controlling the bouncing ball)* And you up there . . . out! *(The arc goes out)* Now let me take this one all by myself, all right? *(The* BOYS *join* BERTHE—*making a chair for her with their arms. They lift her up. She sings)*
Oh, it's time to keep livin'
Time to keep takin' from the world I'm given
You are my time, so I'll throw off my shawl
And watching your flings be flung all over
Makes me feel young all over

BERTHE and BOYS   *(Sing)*
In just no time at all . . .

(The BOYS *carry* BERTHE *offstage and she shouts to* PIPPIN*)*

Remember that, Pippin!

(The screen goes out and PIPPIN *turns to the audience)*

PIPPIN   She's absolutely right. It's time for me to start living . . . and stop worrying. Maybe that's the secret. Just to enjoy all of the simple things in life. The fresh air. *(He takes off his shirt)* The cool, clean water. The fresh fruit off of the . . . *(He reaches for a fruit and the spot reveals a* GIRL *with grapes in her hands and hanging from her breasts. The* GIRL *goes)* Oh yes . . . *(Now the light reveals a terrific-looking* GIRL *at one corner of the stage.* PIPPIN *looks at her.* PIPPIN *looks to the audience*) . . . and women.

   (*The* LEADING PLAYER *enters*)

LEADING PLAYER (*Sings, to the audience, indicating the* GIRL)
   Sex presented pastorally . . .

   (*He goes*)

PIPPIN Of course . . . women . . . (*He sings to the* GIRL)
   My days are brighter than morning air
   Evergreen pine and autumn blue
   But all my days were twice as fair
   If I could share
   My days with you

   (*A light now reveals another* GIRL *and* PIPPIN *goes to her. To the first* GIRL) Excuse me.

   (*Now with the next* GIRL)

   My nights are warmer than firecoals
   Incense and stars and smoke bamboo
   But nights were warm beyond compare

   (*His attention is drawn from one* GIRL *to another by the latter's stimulating caress, and he addresses this Girl now*)

   If I could share
   My nights with you

PIPPIN'S *campaign promises fade out. The lights*
come up on FASTRADA *and* LEWIS *who have been*
watching some of this scene. She speaks to the au-
dience)

Scene 5:

REVOLUTION

FASTRADA   Terrible. A son speaking against his very own father that way. I'd rather be drawn and quartered than think I was in any way responsible for what happened next. After all, I'm just an ordinary housewife and mother, just like all you housewives and mothers out there. Word had come to me that Pippin was holding secret meetings . . . of a treasonous nature.

(Lights down on FASTRADA and LEWIS. PIPPIN'S followers enter. They are wearing cloaks)

MAN 1   Revolution!

MAN 2   Revolution!

MAN 3   Revolution!

MAN 4   Follow Pippin!

MAN 5   We pledge to stand by Pippin . . . forever!

ALL   *(Putting hands together in pledge)* Forever!

(PIPPIN enters)

PIPPIN   Now gentlemen, first, let me say that I admire the dedication and the courage which has brought you here this evening.

ALL   Forever!

PIPPIN   Thank you. Second, let me be honest about some of the dangers which may lie ahead. If, during this insurrection, any one of us is caught, the king's vengeance will be swift and terrible. *(During the course of the following speech, one by one,* ALL *of the* MEN *leave quietly without* PIPPIN'S *knowledge)* You will undoubtedly be tortured ... broken on the wheel ... cruelly maimed ... even dismembered ... But I am sure that the prospect of these terrible agonies will not deter you from joining me in ... *(He turns around and sees that they are gone. Then, to the audience)* They may appear frightened now. But once the deed is done ... once action against the king is taken, they will flock to my side ... maybe.

(He goes. Lights up again on FASTRADA *and* LEWIS. *They gasp in horror over what they have just heard)*

FASTRADA and LEWIS   Oh!

LEWIS   Mama ... if Pippin kills Father ...

FASTRADA   You'll be next in line for the throne, ... darling.

LEWIS   But if Father discovers Pippin's plot and executes him ...

FASTRADA   You'll be next in line for the throne, darling ...

LEWIS   Mama, no matter what happens, I'll move up ...

FASTRADA   Yes, darling.

(Sings)

Back in my younger days, if things were going
   wrong
I might sulk, I might pout
Now I've learned if I just pitch in and do what's right
Things will always work out
And if we all could spread a little sunshine
All could light a little fire
We all would be a little closer
To our heart's desire

(Speaks)

In fear of my beloved husband's life, I brought Pippin's
activities to his attention ... *(Lights up on* CHARLES,
who is standing on a high platform above them) Pippin
is disloyal to you, my lord ...

CHARLES   Every son is disloyal to his father at one
time or another, my lady.

FASTRADA   But Lewis loves you, my lord ...

CHARLES   Lewis is an asshole, my lady.

FASTRADA   *(To audience)* Despite this rejection, I took
upon my tiny shoulders the task of effecting the rap-

prochement between two men for whom I felt . . . deeply. *(Sings)*

> Lord knows we've seen enough troubles already, we've
> Had our fill of grey skies
> So put down the vinegar, take up the honey jar
> You'll catch many more flies
> And if we all could spread a little sunshine
> All could think before we strike
> We all would be a little closer
> To the world we'd like

(Lights up on CHARLES *again)*

My lord?

CHARLES   Yes, my lady?

FASTRADA   Will you be praying at Arles next month?

CHARLES   No, I don't think so.

FASTRADA   Oh, but my lord, you always feel so much better after your yearly prayer.

CHARLES   Yes I do, don't I?

(Lights down on CHARLES)

FASTRADA   I sought out Pippin. *(Lights up on* PIPPIN, *who is atop a platform on the other side of the stage)* Your father loves you, Pippin.

PIPPIN   Freedom and dignity for all men is more important than the love between one father and one son.

FASTRADA   Still, your name will be on his lips when
he prays . . . *(Pause)* . . . at Arles next month.

*(During this exchange, the eyes on the faces in
the backdrop start to move, and they follow the
dialogue from* PIPPIN *to* FASTRADA *and back
again)*

PIPPIN   He prays at Arles next month?

FASTRADA   Alone and unguarded.

PIPPIN   Alone and unguarded. What date?

FASTRADA   The fifteenth.

PIPPIN   What time?

FASTRADA   When the cock crows. *(The eyes on the
backdrop roll)* Pippin, Pippin, I beg you to bring this
estrangement to an end.

PIPPIN   I intend to.

FASTRADA   May I tell your father of this resolve?

PIPPIN   No, no, no, no. Let it be a surprise.

FASTRADA   A surprise. *(To audience)* Isn't that sweet?
(To PIPPIN*)* Your intentions make me very happy. . .

PIPPIN   You've been a great help to me, Fastrada.

(Lights down on PIPPIN *as* FASTRADA *and* LEWIS
dance downstage laughing)

FASTRADA   Oh, what sweeter word could a mother hear. *(Sings)*

    I know the parables told in the Holy Book
    I keep close on my shelf
    God's wisdom teaches me when I help others, I'm
    Really helping myself
    And if we all could spread a little sunshine
    All could lend a helping hand
    We all would be a little closer
    To the promised land
    Closer, closer, closer, closer
    Closer, closer, closer, closer . . .

(FASTRADA and LEWIS dance a few steps, then she speaks to the audience)

It later occurred to me that Pippin might be planning to harm my Charles. I therefore decided to warn him . . .

(Lights up on CHARLES)

CHARLES   Well, I'm off to Arles to pray.

FASTRADA   *(Bows low)* Good-bye, my lord . . . *(CHARLES goes. FASTRADA and LEWIS continue their movements across the stage. Then, suddenly stopping)* Oh dear. In the hustle and bustle of my lord's departure I completely forgot to warn him . . . (She and LEWIS snap their fingers) Oh, my what a busy day . . . (She sends LEWIS off and he exits)* Events move so swiftly it's hard for a simple woman like me to keep up. But something tells me that one day . . . soon . . . I will be able to say what every mother wants to say . . . 'My son, the King'

(At this point, a crown is lowered in and FAS-
TRADA *takes the crown and does a dance with it
When it is over she sings)*

And if we all could spread a little sunshine
All could lend a helping hand
We all would be a little closer
To the promised land
Doo doo doo doo doo doo doo doo doo doo
Doo doo doo doo doo doo doo doo doo doo
    (Speaks) After all, I'm just an ordinary housewife
and mother, just like all you housewives and mothers
out there . . . *(Sings)*
    Doo doo doo doo doo doo doo doo doo doo

*(She dances off, waving good-bye to the audience.
As the lights fade on her and the set goes out, the
set for the chapel comes in and a light comes on
the* LEADING PLAYER)

LEADING PLAYER *(Sings)*
Intrigue—plots to bring disaster . . .
    (Speaks) The chapel at Arles.

(He goes. Lights up on CHARLES, MONKS, *and*
PIPPIN *who is dressed as a monk.)*

CHARLES *(Sensing his presence)* It's all right, Father.
You may come in.

PIPPIN I'm sorry to disturb you, my son. I know you
like to pray alone.

CHARLES You know who I am, Father?

PIPPIN   Of course, my son.

CHARLES   You want something from me perhaps ...
a favor ... advancement?

PIPPIN   No.

CHARLES   Then what, Father?

PIPPIN   I'm here to be with you for one moment ...
to touch you ... to look in your eyes.

CHARLES   And what do you see?

PIPPIN   Two eyes ... a little cloudy with age ... a
sunset.

CHARLES   What else?

PIPPIN   The death of thousands ... the slavery of
more ... terror and bloodshed.

CHARLES   You see that in my eyes?

PIPPIN   Do you deny it?

CHARLES   Deny it? I'm proud of it. I brought order
out of chaos. If slavery, blood, and death are part of
that order ... so be it.

PIPPIN   But those are words from the past. Time has
passed you by, my son.

CHARLES   And your time has come ... my son?

PIPPIN *(Taking down the hood on his robe)* Yes,
Father.

CHARLES It's easy from where you stand to judge the
things that I have done. But when I marched the dust
of the road was in my nose and when I fought the
blood of the enemy was in my eyes. I sank in the mud
on the shores of the Volga. I drowned two legions in
the Vistula. Why eagles, ospreys, even vultures had a
better view. From the heights all things are very clear.
Birds float on the wind. But, by God, I blew my breath
across a continent and shaped an empire with it. Now
if you have no further business with me, go and leave
me to my prayers.

PIPPIN What do you pray for, Father?

CHARLES Strength. And may God give you the same.

(PIPPIN *strikes.* CHARLES *slowly sinks to the
ground, the knife in his back. The* MONKS *who
have been praying softly throughout the scene
laugh quietly. One by one they blow out their
candles as the lights go out on the chapel backdrop)*

PIPPIN *(Sings)*
Why won't my hand stop shaking
When all the earth is still
When ancient ghosts are waking
Many steps need taking
So many plans need making
I think I will
I think I will

(The LEADING PLAYER enters. The MONKS rise and bow to PIPPIN)

MONK 1   Your Majesty.

MONK 2   King Pippin.

MONK 3   Your Majesty.

MONK 4   Your Highness.

MONK 5   King Pippin.

PIPPIN   King Pippin ... *(Sings)*
Morning glow, morning glow
Starts to glimmer when you know
Winds of change are set to blow
And sweep this whole land through
Morning glow is long past due

(As the song progresses, the lights reveal a new backdrop which, at the end, is brilliantly lit as if to suggest a new hope. The rest of the PLAYERS now enter and sing)

ALL   *(Sing)*
Ah

PIPPIN   *(Sings)*
Morning glow fill the earth
Come and shine for all you're worth
We'll be present at the birth
Of old faith looking new
Morning glow is long past due

ALL   *(Sings)*
  Oh, morning glow, I'd like to help you grow

PIPPIN   *(Sings)*
  We should have started long ago

ALL   *(Sing)*
  Ah

PIPPIN and ALL   *(Sing)*
  So, morning glow all day long
  While we sing tomorrow's song
  Never knew we could be so strong
  But now it's very clear

PIPPIN   *(Sings)*
  Morning glow is almost here

  Morning glow by your light
  We can make the new day bright
  And the phantoms of the night
  Will fade into the past
  Morning glow is here

PIPPIN and ALL   *(Sing)*
  At last

LEADING PLAYER   Long live the king!

ALL   *(Sarcastically)* Long live the king.

  (The LEADING PLAYER *puts the crown on* PIP-PIN'S *head. It is much too big, however, and falls over* PIPPIN'S *eyes)*

PIPPIN   *(Groping around)* I think it's a little big.

LEADING PLAYER   *(Taking the crown from* PIPPIN*)* Well, a little tissue paper ought to fix that right up. *(In the following speech, the* MONKS *slip out of their robes and are now in their* PLAYERS' *costumes again. The* LEADING PLAYER *calls out)* King Pippin, Emperor of the Holy Roman Empire . . . (PIPPIN *looks at him excitedly)* . . . is prepared to hear petitions.

PIPPIN   Come ahead. You will all be dealt with fairly. My invitation extends to high and low alike.

   (A BEGGAR *kneels in the light)*

BEGGAR   Sire, I am a poor man . . .

PIPPIN   You may stand. You may all stand . . .

   (They ALL *stand)*

BEGGAR   Thank you, sire. I am a very poor man. I can't find work. You have much and I have nothing. Is that fair?

PIPPIN   No. That's completely unfair. Treasurer? (TREASURER *steps into the light)* I order you to distribute money to the poor . . .

   (They ALL *applaud as the* BEGGAR *thanks him)*

LEADING PLAYER   *(Indicating* PIPPIN'S *future billing)* King Pippin, the Charitable . . .

   (Lights up on a PEASANT*)*

PEASANT   Sire, I'm a peasant. A simple working man. I own not one millimeter of land on which I've worked so hard all my life. Is that fair?

PIPPIN   No. That's terrible. But I will do something about it. I hereby decree that from now on all peasants will own the land that they cultivate.

(They ALL *applaud*)

LEADING PLAYER   King Pippin, the Just ...

(*Lights up on a* NOBLE)

NOBLE   Sire, now that you've given the land to the peasants, we loyal nobles have no source of income. Therefore, we can no longer pay taxes.

PIPPIN   Well, then I hereby abolish taxes.

(They ALL *applaud*)

SOLDIER   You realize sire without taxes you'll have no money to support an army.

PIPPIN   That's all right. I don't need an army. That's it. No more taxes, no more army.

(They ALL *applaud*)

LEADING PLAYER   King Pippin, the Peaceful ...

(FIELD MARSHALL *enters*)

FIELD MARSHALL   Sire, it is my duty to inform you that the Infidel Hun has attacked in the East.

PLAYERS   Oh!

FIELD MARSHALL   He has destroyed three villages . . .

PLAYERS   Oh!

FIELD MARSHALL   . . . raped hundreds of women . . .

PLAYERS   *(Clinging together in horror)* Oh!

FIELD MARSHALL   Tortured and murdered thousands of your royal subjects.

PLAYERS   Oh!

PIPPIN   Can he do that?

FIELD MARSHALL   He has. *(They* ALL *turn to* PIPPIN*)* But he will withdraw . . . on one condition.

PIPPIN   Well, that's very reasonable. I'm certainly willing to make any small concession. What's the condition?

FIELD MARSHALL   He demands your head on a pike-staff.

PIPPIN   Oh. Well, in that case, I guess you'll just have to go out and destroy the Infidel.

FIELD MARSHALL   But sire, I have no more men to wage a campaign . . . I have no money to buy supplies . . . I have no army.

PIPPIN   Excuse me a moment. Nobles? *(Lights up on the* NOBLE *as* PIPPIN *crosses to him)* You remember that decree I made a little while ago about land and taxes?

NOBLE   Yes, sire.

PIPPIN   That's off.

NOBLE   You mean you want me to pay taxes again and raise an army?

PIPPIN   Yes. That's right.

NOBLE   But sire, without land I have neither money nor power over the peasants.

PIPPIN   Oh, yes, that's a very good point *(Stopping for a moment)* I hereby suspend land reform.

   (Lights up on PEASANT*)*

PEASANT   Suspend land reform? Why the hell should I work when the poor get handouts from the royal treasury?

PIPPIN   You're absolutely right. I hereby revoke charity to the poor.

BEGGAR   Up thine, sire.

PIPPIN   Take that man away and hang him! *(The* BEGGAR *puts the noose around his own neck, as the* LEADING PLAYER *starts to take him away. The other* PLAYERS *laugh to themselves)* No. Stop! Wait! Could you just let me think a minute ... please ...

FASTRADA *(Coming to* PIPPIN*)* Darling, you're a born ruler. You're doing a wonderful job. Nothing has changed since your father died. Now about my royal allowance . . .

(All the PLAYERS *close in on* PIPPIN *now with their demands: "Sire, I am a poor man" . . . "Sire, I am a peasant . . ." "Sire I am a . . ." until they're all lined up on the light curtain ad libbing their demands* PIPPIN *is becoming more and more confused)*

PIPPIN Denied. *(Then yelling)* Denied! Denied! Denied!

(They stop)

FASTRADA King Pippin the Unpopular.

PIPPIN Get out of my chapel. I want to pray.

(They ALL *leave, laughing under their breath, as the* LEADING PLAYER *blows out the candles on the altar and goes to* PIPPIN*)*

LEADING PLAYER Pray? You're the king. What would you pray for?

PIPPIN Strength.

(All the PLAYERS *have backed out of the chapel, leaving only* PIPPIN *and the* HEADLESS MAN *who has entered unseen. The* LEADING PLAYER *hovers at the proscenium)*

HEADLESS MAN   Hello.

PIPPIN   Hello.

HEADLESS MAN   I hear you've become king.

PIPPIN   That's right.

HEADLESS MAN   I was wondering ... since you're the king, now ... could you put this back on my shoulders? *(He holds out his head)*

PIPPIN   I'm sorry. I don't think I can.

HEADLESS MAN   Some king.

PIPPIN   There are certain things I just can't do.

HEADLESS MAN   Never mind. I knew you'd be just like the others.

PIPPIN   You don't understand. It's not that easy ...

HEADLESS MAN   They all say that.

(He goes. PIPPIN looks around a moment and goes to CHARLES' body and kneels.)

PIPPIN   Excuse me. Could I have my knife back?

CHARLES   Help yourself.

(CHARLES' hand is seen reaching around and taking the knife out of his back, coming back to life. PIPPIN gives his father the robe, and places the crown over the knife in CHARLES' hand.)

PIPPIN   I'm sorry, Father.

CHARLES   Oh, that's all right, son. Only don't let it happen again.

    (CHARLES *goes.* PIPPIN *looks after him a moment. Then he turns to the* LEADING PLAYER)

PIPPIN   Well, dammit! Nothing turns out the way I thought it would. *(The music for* ON THE RIGHT TRACK *begins, and the* LEADING PLAYER *moves to* PIPPIN) I'm getting old. Very old. And I still haven't done anything with my life.

LEADING PLAYER   But you will. You will.

Scene 6:

ENCOURAGEMENT

LEADING PLAYER   You will.

(Sings)

You look frenzied, you look frazzled
Piqued as any alp
Flushed and rushed and razzle-dazzled
Dry your lips, damp your scalp
Now I can see you're in a rut in
Disarray
And I'm not one to butt in
But in fact I must say
If you'd take it easy, trust awhile
Don't look blue, don't look back
You'll pull through in just awhile
'Cause you're on the right track

PIPPIN *(Sings)*	LEADING PLAYER *(Sings)*
On the right track	Uh hu hu hu
On the right track	Take it easy, sonny
On the right track	Take it easy, sonny
On the right track	Take it easy

LEADING PLAYER   *(Sings)*
Why be flurried

PIPPIN   *(Sings)*
  Flustered

LEADING PLAYER   *(Sings)*
  Keep those

PIPPIN   *(Sings)*
  Hopes aloft

LEADING PLAYER   *(Sings)*
  Keep cool as custard

PIPPIN   *(Sings)*
  Trying hard

LEADING PLAYER   *(Sings)*
  Stepping soft

BOTH   *(Sing)*
  There's no trick to staying sensible
  Despite each cul-de-sac
  'Cause each step indispensible
  When you're on the right track

PIPPIN   *(Sings)*   LEADING PLAYER   *(Sings)*
  On the right track   The right track
  On the right track   Take it easy, sonny
  On the right track   Take it easy, sonny
  On the right track   Take it easy

(The song develops into a dance during which the LEADING PLAYER *encourages* PIPPIN *to "Go, but easy")*

LEADING PLAYER   Pippin jumped back into life with
his usual zest. He tried art ... the creative life, and
you know something, he wasn't too bad. But what he
discovered was ...

PIPPIN   ... you got to be dead to find out if you were
any good.

LEADING PLAYER   Then he dedicated himself to the
church. He sought God in the highways, he sought
Him in the byways ... and then he finally cornered
Him in a huge cathedral. But what he found out was ...

PIPPIN   The church isn't saving souls, it's investing in
real estate.

LEADING PLAYER   *(Sings)*
    Many when things get dank will
    Feel their grip go
    We stay tranquil,
    Spirits high, pulses low

PIPPIN   *(Sings, coming through light curtain again. It
goes out, as the scrim comes in)*
    But! What I've left behind looks trifling
    What's ahead looks black
    Am I doomed to spend my life a-lingering on

LEADING PLAYER   *(Sings)*
    Lingering on

PIPPIN   *(Sings)*
    Just lingering on

BOTH *(Sing)*
  Malingering on the right

PIPPIN Oh, I'll never find it ... never ... never ...
never ... never! Shit!

  (He collapses in a heap)

LEADING PLAYER Easy ...

  (Sings)

  You're on the right track!

                BLACK OUT

Scene 7:

THE HEARTH

LEADING PLAYER *(Appearing from one of the side platforms)* Enter ... Catherine. *(The lights come up on* TWO PLAYERS *holding a scarf. They lower to reveal* CATHERINE. *But there is no* CATHERINE. *The* PLAYERS *look in the wings for her, and back to the* LEADING PLAYER. *He tries once more)* Enter ... Catherine!

(CATHERINE *enters in a hurry)*

CATHERINE *(To the* LEADING PLAYER*)* Sorry ... I couldn't get my eyelash on ...

LEADING PLAYER It's okay. We'll just try it again. *(*CATHERINE *goes behind the scarf)* Enter ... Catherine. *(The scarf is lowered and* CATHERINE *turns around)* A widow with a small boy and a large estate.

(He goes)

CATHERINE *(To audience, as she goes to* PIPPIN *who is lying on the stage)* When I first saw Pippin he was lying in the road like a discarded rag. I would have passed him by.

(Sings)

Perhaps I should have passed him by
But there was something about his foot
Yes ... it was the arch of his foot
That caught my eye

(Speaks)

What I did was merely an act of Christian charity. After all, I had no idea that this discarded rag would clean up so well.

(She motions to the TWO PLAYERS *who place* PIPPIN *in the bed which was set behind the scrim upstage, while she sings)*

There he was
He didn't know where he was
And he looked so lost and exhausted
You'd almost swear he was dead
So I said:
Pick him up, put him to bed
See that he's bathed and clothed and fed
As I said, How could I foretell
He'd clean up, oh, so very well
Imagine my surprise
When I raised my eyes
And there he was

(Speaks)

The man had obviously lost the will to live. So the first thing I had to do was to get him interested in something ... something that would restore his faith in life ... something like ... me *(Going upstage to* PIPPIN*)* Well Pippin, I'm sure there are many things you'd like to know about me, aren't there?

PIPPIN   No

CATHERINE   Good. *(Music under)* My name is Catherine. I'm a widow. I have a son. I own this estate.

(Sings)

> I'm your everyday, customary kind of woman
> Practical as salt
> Modest to a fault
> Conservative with a budget
> Liberal with a meal
> Just your average ideal
>
> My telling you this
> May seem sudden and strange
> It may not interest you much at all right now
> But things change
> Things change
>
> Still I'll understand if I'm not your kind of woman
> Anyone can make
> One terrible mistake
> And I've no special glamour
> No bait I can twirl
> For I'm just a plain, everyday
> Commonplace, come-what-may
> Average, ordinary
> Wonderful girl!

(Looking at him, then speaks to the audience)

God! What a challenge! For a long time he showed no interest in anything. I was determined to somehow pierce that dedicated apathy. Now ... I've always found that no man ... no matter what his condition ... can resist the charm of a small boy. So, I sent my son Theo to him . . .

(THEO'S *entrance music. The* LEADING PLAYER *enters carrying* THEO *and his* DUCK)

LEADING PLAYER   Enter Theo. A small lovable boy and his large lovable duck.

(LEADING PLAYER *snaps his fingers and goes*)

THEO   (*Trying to wake* PIPPIN *up*) Pippin . . . Pippin . . . say hello to my duck . . . (*He pushes the* DUCK *into* PIPPIN'S *face*)

PIPPIN   How do you do . . .

THEO   Guess his name.

PIPPIN   Augustus.

THEO   Wrong. His name's Otto. You're not very smart . . .

PIPPIN   I am smart enough to know that a duck belongs in a pond and not in my bed!

(THEO *looks at* PIPPIN *a moment, then gives him a juicy "raspberry" and goes.* PIPPIN *tries to go back to sleep*)

CATHERINE   (*Who has been observing all of this from downstage*) Obviously hopeless. I had picked him up off the road. I could throw him back out again. Out he goes! (*Goes to* PIPPIN, *and is again stunned by the beauty of his foot. The anger drains out of her*) I'll give him another chance. (*To* PIPPIN) Pippin, you have been lying in this bed for seven days, now what is the matter with you?

PIPPIN Well it's nothing you could possibly understand ...

CATHERINE Well, try me. Give me a chance.

PIPPIN All right. You see, I have an overwhelming need to be completely fulfilled. And it's never ever happened to me so I am in abject despair.

CATHERINE And that's it?

PIPPIN Yes. That's it.

CATHERINE (*Coming downstage, to audience*) You may think that what I did next was scheming ... devious ... (*Turns back to* PIPPIN) Pippin, let me tell you something about despair. (*She points to the conductor and the organ begins to play as if this were the beginning of a soap opera.* PIPPIN *is surprised by the music and begins to search for its source.* CATHERINE *sits on the end of the bed and begins speaking*) I loved my husband very much. The years we spent together were the happiest years of my life. And then one day he was struck by fever ... (*Slowly* PIPPIN *comes down to the end of the bed and watches her*) ... and when his hand went cold in mine, I felt my life, too, was over. I was overcome by the deepest despair. I took to my bed for five days. On the sixth day I got up. There were things to be done. An estate to be run. A boy to raise. (*The organ plays a grand finish.* CATHERINE *looks to the audience and smiles.* PIPPIN *is staring at her. To audience*) Well, look at that. I think he's really moved. (PIPPIN *reaches out and touches* CATHERINE'S *hand.*

She looks at the hand for a long moment. Then, softly, to PIPPIN) Pippin, this is such a large estate. I'm all alone here and I can't do all this work by myself. Couldn't you please help me ...

PIPPIN   All right! All right! *(He starts to go)* But just for a little while ...

   (Goes. CATHERINE *moves downstage and the bed revolves. It is now a tree)*

CATHERINE   *(To audience)* Well, Pippin was finally out of bed and working ... and slowly he became part of everything ... part of our everyday life ...

   (A musical vamp begins and PIPPIN *enters between* TWO MEN, *one of whom is the* LEADING PLAYER, *disguised as a worker. They cross the stage rhythmically, mechanically, each with a hoe. Together, they move across the stage as if they were hoeing the fields.* PIPPIN *addresses the two men as* CATHERINE *watches)*

PIPPIN   How often do we do this?

LEADING PLAYER   Every day ...

PIPPIN   Every day?

MEN   Uh huh.

PIPPIN   Every day. That's exciting. *(Sees* CATHERINE *looking at him)* Did you say something?

CATHERINE   No, no ...

(She goes, PIPPIN *looks after her as the* TWO MEN
go off. Then, to the audience)

PIPPIN   I know that look. That's the look of a widow
with a small boy and a large estate and nobody to sit at
the head of the table.

(He goes)

CATHERINE   *(Coming back onstage)* For awhile, Pippin didn't show much enthusiasm for the work . . . but
as time went on . . . (PIPPIN *and the* TWO MEN *enter.
This time they cross the stage in the same rhythmic
pattern, only this time they have seed bags and are
sowing the fields.* PIPPIN *is totally unenthusiastic, and
he throws the seeds from his bag into the bag of one of
the other* MEN) . . . he showed no enthusiasm at all.

PIPPIN   *(Letting the* MAN *pass him by and sending
him off with a pat on the behind, calls after them)*
Keep up the good work, boys. *(Seeing* CATHERINE
watching him) Well, what are you looking at?

CATHERINE   Nothing . . . nothing . . . (PIPPIN *starts to
go)* Oh Pippin, there is something. The roof on the
chicken house—it's sprung a leak . . . if you could get
to it tomorrow . . .

PIPPIN   Wait a minute . . .

CATHERINE   . . . or the day after tomorrow.

(She goes)

PIPPIN   *(To himself)* The roof on the chicken house
. . .? *(Calling after her)* I used to be the emperor of

the Holy Roman Empire ... *(To audience)* All right,
so I screwed it up. Still ...

(Sings)

Patching the roof and pitching the hay
Is not my idea of a perfect day
When you're extraordinary
You gotta do extraordinary things

I'm not the type who loses sleep
Over the size of the compost heap
When you're extraordinary
You think about extraordinary things

That's the reason I'll never be
The kind of man who dwells
On how moths got into the tapestry
Or why the dungeon smells

Oh, it's hard to feel special, it's hard to feel big
Feeding the turtle and walking the pig
It's so secondary
To someone who is very
Extraordinary like me

If the moat won't stop leaking
And the goat won't stop shrieking
And the griffin keeps losing its hair
If the west wing is rotting
And our best wine is clotting
Well, I'm terribly sorry but I don't care

I've got to be someone who lives
All of his life in superlatives
When you're extraordinary
You gotta do extraordinary things

The fact that I'm special is easy to see
So why doesn't anybody know it but me?
I'm extraordinary
I need to do extraordinary things

Every so often a man has a day
He truly can call his
Well, here I am to seize my day
If someone would just tell me when the hell it is

Oh give me my chance, and give me my wings
And don't make me think about everyday things
They're unnecessary
To someone who is very
Extraordinary
Like me!

(Speaks) I am. I am extraordinary. I am. (CATHER-
INE *enters)* That's it! I'm leaving. I'm getting out ...
tomorrow!

CATHERINE *(To audience)* And then Theo's duck
got sick.

> (THEO *enters and goes to* PIPPIN. *He has the* DUCK
> *in his arms)*

THEO   Pippin ... Pippin, Otto is sick.

> *(During this scene,* CATHERINE *stands behind* PIP-
> PIN *and* THEO. *Her remarks, though directed to*
> PIPPIN *and* THEO, *are unheard by them)*

PIPPIN   That's too bad, Theo. I'm sorry.

CATHERINE   Pippin, it's the first time he's come to
you for help ...

THEO   Could you look at him ... please ...

CATHERINE   Please ... Pippin.

PIPPIN   Theo, I don't know anything about ducks ...

CATHERINE   Pippin ... try ...

PIPPIN   Oh, all right. Let me have a look at him.

(He takes the DUCK *reluctantly and looks at it for a long moment)*

CATHERINE   Now say something hopeful ...

PIPPIN   *(Giving the* DUCK *back to* THEO*)* This is a very sick duck. There's nothing I can do for him. (THEO *starts to go away with the* DUCK. *He is very sad.* PIPPIN *looks after him.)* Oh, Theo, yes there is. *(Rising to get* THEO.*)* Wait a minute. Come here. Come and kneel down here next to me. Right over here. (PIPPIN *and* THEO *kneeling next to one another, pray)*

CATHERINE   It was like a painting. Man and boy at prayer.

PIPPIN   God, I know this is going to sound ridiculous, but this boy loves this duck ...

(Sings)

His breath has ebbed, his pulse is low
His feet are webbed, but even so
You must know
That although our tears are poised to burst

We've kept our faith warm through the worst
We haven't cursed our luck or run amuck
To prayer we've stuck
Please reward our pluck
And save this duck

CATHERINE *(To audience)* They prayed all day. And then, just after sunset ... *(Light goes out on the* DUCK*)* ... the duck died ...

PIPPIN I'm sorry, Theo ... (THEO, *obviously heart-broken, takes the* DUCK *in his arms and goes)* Wait a minute, Theo. We can go to the pond and get another duck. *(But this has no effect.* THEO *is gone.* PIPPIN *turns to* CATHERINE*)* Why did the Goddamn duck have to die?

(He goes)

CATHERINE *(To audience)* Then, an interesting thing happened. Theo plunged himself into monumental despair. While on the other hand, Pippin, that Prince of Despair, dedicated himself to raising the boy's spirits ...

*(*THEO *enters with his head way down looking very sad.* PIPPIN *enters following* THEO *and a little too cheerful)*

PIPPIN Theo! Hey, Theo, look, we're going out to thresh some grain right now and we need another good man. You want to give us a helping hand? (THEO *exits paying no attention)* Another time, maybe ...

(Goes)

CATHERINE But Pippin showed remarkable persistence. When one thing failed he tried another.

PIPPIN *(From offstage)* Theo ... hey, Theo ... (THEO *enters whittling a stick.* PIPPIN *enters on a pair of stilts)* Want to be the tallest little boy in the world? *(Walking on the stilts to where* THEO *is sitting)* Fee, fie, foe, fun. I smell the blood ... *(He gets off stilts and offers them to* THEO*)* Here I made you a pair of stilts. Come on, I'll help you up. You can be taller ... (THEO *rises and crosses downstage where he sits with his back toward* PIPPIN) ... than anybody.

(Seeing that it's no use, PIPPIN *takes the stilts and goes upstage behind the tree)*

CATHERINE *(To audience)* Well, most men would have given up. But Pippin, with amazing perseverance tried yet another way.

*(*PIPPIN *enters from behind the tree. This time he has a small baby lamb)*

PIPPIN Theo, guess what I have for you this time. Now don't turn around. I'm going to bring it right down to you ... *(he goes to* THEO*)* Okay, when I count to three you can turn around and look. One! Two! Three! Look!

*(*THEO *turns around. Looks at the lamb, then at* PIPPIN*)*

THEO That's not a duck, dummy!

(He goes)

PIPPIN   *(Dejectedly)* Did I say it was a duck? *(To the lamb)* Yeah, go on . . . you were a flop.

> (PIPPIN *exits with the lamb. He comes back on shaking his head apologetically and crosses the stage.*
>
> *As he passes* CATHERINE, *she stops him and pulls him close to her. She takes his face in her hands and kisses him tenderly.*
>
> *Romantic music creeps in.*
>
> CATHERINE *kisses* PIPPIN *again, and this time he responds.*
>
> *The tree revolves upstage, and becomes a bed again.*
>
> CATHERINE *and* PIPPIN, *looking at each other, go up to either side of the bed.*
>
> *As they do, the lights fade and the music changes tone . . . from romantic to corny passionate.*
>
> *Then* TWO DANCERS, *a* MAN *and a* WOMAN *appear at opposite sides of the stage. They are scantily dressed and they execute seductive, erotic movements directed at each other.*
>
> *Finally, as the music reaches a climax, the* WOMAN, *full of confidence, makes an extraordinary leap for the* MAN.
>
> *The* MAN *misjudges the angle of the leap and bungles the catch. They both fall to the ground in an ungainly sprawl.*
>
> *Lights come up on the bed.* PIPPIN *and* CATHERINE *are sitting up. They are grim)*

PIPPIN   *(After a long pause)* I'm sorry.

CATHERINE   I'm sorry.

PIPPIN   No, no. It was my fault.

CATHERINE   It was my fault. It's been a long time for me ...

PIPPIN   No, no ... I just forgot ... oh ... *(They are silent for a moment)* You know, I think ...

CATHERINE   Yes ...?

PIPPIN   It'll be better ...

CATHERINE   *(Hopefully)* Next time?

PIPPIN   Next time.

> *(Lights down on the bed. The* TWO DANCERS *return and execute a similar dance. Again the music reaches a climax and the* WOMAN *prepares for the extraordinary leap. The* MAN *braces to catch her.*
> *The* WOMAN *is in the air ... and this time the* MAN *catches her with effortless grace.*
> *Lights up on the bed.* PIPPIN *and* CATHERINE *are sitting up, smiling broadly.*
> *The bed revolves into the tree and the* LEADING PLAYER *comes from behind it and addresses the audience)*

LEADING PLAYER   Listen, I think we're gonna skip part of this. Nothing much really happens. A little bit of this, a little bit of that ... *(And then referring to the bed upstage)* ... a whole lot of *that.* (PIPPIN *and* CATHERINE *come around the bed now, and start to move downstage)* But, the season changed as it always

does, and the days were filled with those everyday
things. Seeds to be sown ... fences to be mended ...
and, finally, of course, a love song to be sung.

(CATHERINE *and* PIPPIN *are seated on the floor
center stage. The* LEADING PLAYER *goes*)

CATHERINE   (*Sings*)

PIPPIN   (*Sings*)
 Sitting on the floor and talking 'til dawn

 Candles and confidences

PIPPIN   (*Sings*)
 Trading old beliefs and humming old songs

CATHERINE   (*Sings*)
 And lowering old defenses

PIPPIN   (*Sings*)
 Singing a

BOTH   (*Sing*)
 Love song—la la la la la la la la la lá
 Love song—la la la la

PIPPIN   (*Sings*)
 Private little jokes and silly pet names

CATHERINE   (*Sings*)
 Lavender soap and lotions

PIPPIN   (*Sings*)
 All of the cliches and all of the games

CATHERINE *(Sings)*
And all of the strange emotions

PIPPIN *(Sings)*
Singing a

BOTH *(Sing)*
Love song—la la la la la la la la la la
Love song—la la la la la

PIPPIN *(Sings)*
They say the whole is greater

BOTH *(Sing)*
Than the sum of the parts it's made of

PIPPIN *(Sings)*
Well if it's true of anything

BOTH *(Sing)*
It's true of love

PIPPIN *(Sings)*
Cause how can you define a look or a touch?

CATHERINE *(Sings)*
How can you weigh a feeling?

PIPPIN *(Sings)*
Taken by themselves now they don't mean much

BOTH *(Sing)*
Together they send you reeling

PIPPIN *(Sings)*
Into a

BOTH   *(Sing)*
   Love song—la la la la la la la la la la la la
   Love song—la la la la la
   La la la la la la la la la la
   La la la la la la la la la la

CATHERINE   *(Speaks)*
   Close your eyes.

PIPPIN   Why?

CATHERINE   Because we've got a surprise for you.

   (THEO, *who has entered quietly, now runs to*
   PIPPIN *and throws his arms around* PIPPIN'S
   neck)

THEO   We've got a surprise!

CATHERINE and THEO   We've got a surprise!

(The tree-unit revolves, and this time the bed has
been converted into a dining room table set with
dishes and food. From the wings, a few of the
PLAYERS *enter with stools and place them around*
the table. After this is done, they exit.
   CATHERINE *helps* PIPPIN *up and leads* PIPPIN *to*
the table. THEO *clings to* PIPPIN)

CATHERINE   Keep your eyes closed, Pippin. Now no
peeking.

PIPPIN   I usually don't like surprises.

CATHERINE   Well, you'll like this one.

(They have reached the table, and CATHERINE *and* THEO *help* PIPPIN *to a seat)*

PIPPIN   Can I open my eyes, please?

CATHERINE   Yes, now you can. (PIPPIN *opens his eyes.* CATHERINE *uncovers a dish and lights the contents)* Quince pudding flambé! Oh, I haven't made it for years ... but I thought that for this special occasion ...

PIPPIN   What special occasion?

CATHERINE   Well ... six months ago today ... *(Pause)* ... you arrived here. So Theo and I thought that we would celebrate with a little party. So I made this ... and Theo made you a flute ...

THEO   *(Handing the flute to* PIPPIN) Here.

PIPPIN   Oh, Theo ... it's beautiful. Thank you. I don't know what to say.

CATHERINE   Well let me say something then. *(Pause)* In the six months that you've been with us, you've come to mean a great deal to me ... to us ... to our very ordinary lives. So, I just want to say for me ... for Theo ... we're glad you're here. And now ... well, now we have so many good years ahead of us ... *(She and* THEO *move* PIPPIN *to the head of the table.* PIPPIN *sits very reluctantly)* Well, isn't anybody going to eat my pudding?

THEO   I am!

(CATHERINE *starts to dish out the pudding.* PIP-
PIN *rises suddenly, and goes downstage*)

PIPPIN   I've got to get out of here.

CATHERINE   *(Going to him)* ... Pippin, what's the
matter?

PIPPIN   I just can't stay here.

CATHERINE   I don't understand.

PIPPIN   I've got to go.

CATHERINE   Why?

PIPPIN   Because this isn't enough. Life is more than
ducks that die ... and leaking roofs ... and flaming
quince pudding!

CATHERINE   Are you sure?

PIPPIN   Yes I'm sure. And I am not going to be stuck
doing the same damn thing every day ...

CATHERINE   ... and night?

PIPPIN   Don't you see, there has to be something
more than this. There has to be.

CATHERINE   Maybe there isn't any more.

PIPPIN   I know there is.   CATHERINE   *(To audi-*
                                ence, as if a litany,
   (Sings)   *learned by rote)*

Rivers belong where
they can ramble
Eagles belong where
they can fly
I've got to be where my
spirit can run free
Gotta find . . .

I loved my husband very much. The years we spent together were the happiest years of my life. And then one day he was struck by fever . . . and when his hand went cold in mine, I felt my life, too, was over. I was overcome by the deepest despair. I took to my bed for five days. On the sixth day I got up. There were things to be done. An estate to be run. A boy to raise.

(PIPPIN *goes. The lights begin to go out on her*)

CATHERINE   Could you hold the light for a minute . . . please? *(The light comes back on)* Thank you.

(She sings)

I'll guess I'll miss the man
Explain it if you can
His face was far from fine
But still I'll miss his face
And wonder if he's missing mine.

(The LEADING PLAYER *enters behind the scrim. As she continues to sing all of the* PLAYERS, *one by one, enter behind the scrim watching her)*

(Sings)

Some days he wouldn't say
A pleasant word all day
Some days he'd scowl and curse
But there were other days
When he was really ... even worse
Some men are heroes
Some men outshine the sun
Some men are simple, good men
This man wasn't one

And I won't miss his moods
His gloomy solitudes
His blunt abrasive style
But please don't get me wrong
He was the best to come along
In a long, long while ...

(Speaks)

And the arch of his foot really was in a class by itself.

(She goes)

Scene 8:

THE FINALE

The stage is in darkness.
We hear the same orchestral vamp that we heard at the beginning of the show.
The light curtain comes on and we see all the PLAYERS *standing on it singing the low crooning vocal wail.*
PIPPIN is sitting downstage on the floor, looking very discouraged. The PLAYERS *move in around him.*

LEADING PLAYER   Well, Pippin, I guess you finally realize what we knew from the beginning ...

PIPPIN   What's that?

A PLAYER   ... that your search for perfection and fulfillment was doomed from the start.

A PLAYER   Nothing ever turns out the way you think it's going to ...

A PLAYER   It's all flawed in one way or another ...

A PLAYER   Isn't that true?

LEADING PLAYER Nothing has been completely fulfilling now, has it, Pippin? Has it?

PIPPIN No. *(They ALL laugh quietly and nod)* I guess there's nothing.

LEADING PLAYER *(Laughing)* Wait ... wait a minute! There is something ...

PIPPIN There is ...? *(They ALL nod and ad lib "Oh, yes")* What?

LEADING PLAYER The only completely perfect act in our repertoire ... the finale!

ALL *(Screaming and clapping)* The finale!

(A few of the PLAYERS bring on a large set piece which is the trick fire box. The LEADING PLAYER claps and the PLAYER with the torch who appeared briefly in the opening jumps on)

PLAYER Now?

LEADING PLAYER Now.

(The PLAYER with the torch goes upstage to the box. Another PLAYER steps inside the box. A cloth is held up in front of the box which reads "PIPPIN'S GRAND FINALE." The PLAYER with the torch sets fire to a dummy inside the box who is supposed to be a man. The cloth is lowered. We see the dummy burn. After it burns, the cloth is brought up again and the PLAYER steps in front of it. It is a very realistic and frightening trick, and when it is over the troupe applauds)

ALL   Ta da!

PIPPIN   That's the finale? But that was just a trick . . .

LEADING PLAYER   When *he* does it, it's just a trick.
But when you do it, it'll be for real.

PIPPIN   When I do it . . .? *(He looks around at all the*
PLAYERS. *They nod "Yes" to* PIPPIN) You mean you
want me to get into that box and set myself on fire?
(The PLAYERS *begin to close in on* PIPPIN) Wait a
minute . . .

A PLAYER   You will step into that flame, Pippin . . .

LEADING PLAYER   Become part of that flame . . .

A PLAYER   Be engulfed by that flame . . .

A PLAYER   Become flame itself . . .

   (They are all around PIPPIN *now)*

LEADING PLAYER   And for one moment shine with
unequalled brilliance . . .

A PLAYER   And in that flame you'll become a glorious
synthesis of life and death . . .

A PLAYER   . . . and life again . . .

LEADING PLAYER   *(Turns to the audience)* Ladies and
Gentlemen . . . presenting the Great Pippin, in our
grand finale never before seen on a public stage!

(A drum roll begins and they all applaud wildly . . . they are ecstatic with pleasure at the thought of PIPPIN *burning himself)*

PIPPIN   Stop! Stop! Stop that! *(They stop. The drum roll stops)* Look, if this finale is so spectacular, why don't one of you do it?

LEADING PLAYER   *(After a long pause)* Look, we're just ordinary run-of-the-mill people. Just your everyday men and women who keep this old world spinning . . . hell, we're nothing. *(They* ALL *begin to close in on* PIPPIN *again)* But you, Pippin, you're an extraordinary human being . . . with extraordinary aspirations and dreams.

A PLAYER   You deserve an extraordinary climax . . .

A PLAYER   . . . an unparalleled finale . . .

LEADING PLAYER   It's everything you've been looking for . . .

A PLAYER   Your dream!

A PLAYER   Complete ultimate fulfillment!

A PLAYER   Perfection! Like the sun blazing in the sky!

LEADING PLAYER   The sun at its zenith!

(Now the song begins, led by the LEADING PLAYER, *later joined by* ALL. PIPPIN *stares into the flame,*

reluctant at first, but slowly becoming carried away
by the music and the fire)
(Sings)

Think about the sun, Pippin
think about her golden glance
How she lights the world up
Well, now it's your chance
With the guardians of splendor
Inviting you to dance
Pippin
Think about the sun

ALL   *(Ad lib, whispering, beckoning* PIPPIN *to the
fire-box)* Now, Pippin ... come on, Pippin ... it's
ready ...

LEADING PLAYER   Now, Pippin ... it's time.

PIPPIN   Look, it's just that if this *isn't* it ... I'm going
to have a tough time trying something else ...

A PLAYER   Pippin, you lack a certain amount of
poise ...

A PLAYER   Think of the radiance ...

A PLAYER   Remember the beauty ...

A PLAYER   Admiring glances ...

A PLAYER   Thunderous applause ...

A PLAYER   Think of the word-of-mouth ...

LEADING PLAYER   *(Sings)*
 Think about your life, Pippin

FASTRADA   *(Sings)*
 Days are tame and nights the same

LEADING PLAYER   *(Sings)*
 Now think about the beauty

LEADING PLAYER *and* FASTRADA   *(Sing)*
 In one perfect flame

(As the rest of the PLAYERS *join in the song, the final set comes in. It is a backdrop which looks like the sun, shining and brilliant, with angels on it)*

LEADING PLAYER and FASTRADA *(Sing)*	ALL *(Sing)*
And the angels of the morning	Ahhh
Are calling out your name	Ahhh

ALL   *(Sing)*
 Pippin

LEADING PLAYER   *(Sings)*
 Think about the

ALL   *(Sing)*
 Sun

A PLAYER   More lights, perhaps?

LEADING PLAYER   You want more lights, you got 'em! Let's give this angel some light!

(He claps. The lights go on and now the lighting would do justice to only Christ on the cross ... super-religious and dramatic. The music becomes rhythmic, insistent. The PLAYERS add tambourines)

ALL   *(Singing again)*
Think about your life, Pippin
Think about the dreams you planned
Think about the moment
That's so close at hand
When the power and the glory
Are there at your command
Pippin
Think about your life

(The tambourines increase their jiggling, the singing becomes louder and wilder)

Think about the sun, Pippin
Think about her golden glance
How she lights the world up
Well, now it's your chance
With the guardians of splendor
Inviting you to dance
Pippin
Think about the sun

(In the course of the following verse, the unison breaks into harmony. PIPPIN is slowly becoming part of their rhythmic gyrations, his resistance getting lower and lower)

ALL   *(Sing)*
   Think about your life, Pippin
   Think about the dreams you planned
   Think about the moment
   That's so close at hand
   When the power and the glory
   Are there at your command

   When the power and the glory
   Are there at your command
   When the power and the glory
   Are there at your command

   Pippin, think about your life

   (PIPPIN *has the torch now. He looks at it as
   though in a trance, as the* LEADING PLAYER *beck-
   ons him toward the firebox and the* PLAYERS *sing)*

   Rivers belong where they can ramble
   Eagles belong where they can fly . . .

   (PIPPIN *runs up to a* PLAYER *and gives back
   the torch. Ad lib, whispering, beckoning, calling
   to him)*

Pippin . . . Pippin . . . now, Pippin, now . . . come on,
Pippin . . .

PIPPIN   No, stop! Please don't do that to me . . .
please . . .
   (PIPPIN *covers his ears and the noise stops. The*
   PLAYERS *freeze.)*

   (Sings)

I'm not a river or a giant bird
That soars to the sea
And if I'm never tied to anything
I'll never be free

(CATHERINE *and* THEO *enter from behind the fire-box. Slowly,* PIPPIN *turns to them and goes toward them*)

LEADING PLAYER *(To* CATHERINE) What the hell are you doing out here? *(To* PIPPIN) Hey, where are you going, Pippin? Come on, stop this nonsense and get on with ... the finale, Pippin ... the finale ...

ALL *(Ad lib)* The finale, Pippin ... the finale ...

(PIPPIN *takes* CATHERINE *and* THEO *by the hand. They stand together*)

A PLAYER Coward ...

A PLAYER Compromiser ...

ALL Compromiser!

PIPPIN *(Sings)*
 I wanted magic shows and miracles
 Mirages to touch
 I wanted such a little thing from life
 I wanted so much
 I never came close, my love
 We nearly came near
 It never was there
 I think it was here ...

LEADING PLAYER and ALL All right ... you'll see
what it's like without us ... take away the set ... everything out ... move it. *(The set begins to move out)*
Colored lights out. Take 'em out. Pinks and reds out
... well, that's not too flattering is it, Pippin? *(The
lighting becomes harsh.* PIPPIN *does not answer)* Costumes ... get their costumes ... *(The* PLAYERS *strip*
CATHERINE, PIPPIN, *and* THEO, *leaving them in black
tights)* Makeup ... let's go ... get it off ... and the
wigs ... (PLAYERS *remove makeup and wigs from* PIP-
PIN, CATHERINE *and* THEO) Look around, Pippin. How
do things look to you now?

PIPPIN *(Sings)*
    They showed me crimson, gold and lavender
    A shining parade ...

LEADING PLAYER A mole, Pippin. Look at the mole
on her face. You're going to spend the rest of your life
with a woman with a mole?

PIPPIN *(Sings)*
    But there's no color I can have on earth
    That won't finally fade ...

LEADING PLAYER and ALL And the kid ... He'll
whine 24 hours a day ... gimme this! gimme that!

PIPPIN *(Sings)*
    When I wanted worlds to paint

LEADING PLAYER and ALL This is the way you want
to live? Is this what you want?

PIPPIN *(Sings)*
    And costumes to wear ...

LEADING PLAYER   No costumes . . . no makeup . . .

PIPPIN   *(Sings)*
  I think it was here . . .

LEADING PLAYER and ALL   No pink lights . . .

PIPPIN   *(Sings)*
  Cause it never was there . . .

ALL   And no magic!

  (The lights are beginning to go out one by one)

LEADING PLAYER   *(To audience)* Ladies and gentlemen, we apologize for our inability to bring you the finale that we promised. It seems our extraordinary
young man has elected to compromise his aspirations.
But I know there are many of you out there . . . extraordinary people . . . exceptional people . . . who
would gladly trade your ordinary lives for the oppor-
tunity to do one perfect act—our grand finale. Now, if
you should decide to do so, we'll be there for you . . .
waiting . . . anytime you want us. Why we're right inside your heads. And we promise you sets, costumes,
lights, magic . . . and a short—but—spectacular career!
(They ALL *look out to the audience, singling out
people and asking them to come with them)* All right.
Let's go! Out. Everybody out . . . out! *(The* PLAYERS
go) Take out the rest of the lights. *(Lights go out. A
stage manager brings a work light on)* Orchestra, pack
up your fiddles. Get your horns. Let's go *(Then to the
pianist)* Take your damn hands off that keyboard! *(Pi-
ano stops. It is silent. Then, to* PIPPIN) You try singing
without music, sweetheart!

(The LEADING PLAYER *goes. The stage is dark except for the work light.* PIPPIN, CATHERINE, *and* THEO *are alone on stage.* PIPPIN *sings without music)*

PIPPIN   *(Sings)*
  I wanted magic shows and miracles
  Mirages to touch
  I wanted such a little thing from life
  I wanted so much

CATHERINE   Pippin ... do you feel that you've compromised?

PIPPIN   No.

CATHERINE   Do you feel like a coward?

PIPPIN   No.

CATHERINE   How do you feel ...?

PIPPIN   Trapped ... but happy ... *(He looks from one to the other and smiles)* which isn't too bad for the end of a musical comedy. Ta da!

  (They bow as the curtain comes down)